LOVING YOU
COUPON BOOK
PRIORITY

With Love,

From: Ryan

To: Amy

Veronica Rosey

THIS COUPON ENTITLES YOU TO ONE:

WIN THE ARGUMENT

Even if you are wrong 😊.

THIS COUPON ENTITLES YOU TO ONE:

UNBIRTHDAY DAY

We are going to celebrate like it's your Birthday! Cake included!

THIS COUPON ENTITLES YOU TO ONE:

BOYS' NIGHT OUT

No curfew, no checking in.

THIS COUPON ENTITLES YOU TO ONE:

FULL BODY

MASSAGE

Just lay down and enjoy!

THIS COUPON ENTITLES YOU TO ONE:

BUBBLE BATH FOR TWO

Had a rough day? Relax!... Wine included.

THIS COUPON ENTITLES YOU TO ONE:

FANTASY
FULFILLED

Terms: Let me know 24 hours in advance if
you have any special requests.

THIS COUPON ENTITLES YOU TO ONE:

HOMEMADE
DINNER

I'll make the dinner of your choice exactly as you want it.

THIS COUPON ENTITLES YOU TO ONE:

BREAKFAST
IN BED

Terms: Let me know 24 hours in advance.

THIS COUPON ENTITLES YOU TO ONE:

ANYWHERE, ANYTIME

Yep, you read that right! Enjoy!

THIS COUPON ENTITLES YOU TO ONE:

SEXY TEXT

Terms: To be delivered within 24 hours of receiving the request.

THIS COUPON ENTITLES YOU TO ONE:

SPORTS

EVENT

Terms: To be delivered within 3 weeks of receiving the request.

THIS COUPON ENTITLES YOU TO ONE:

GAME NIGHT

Board games, video games, sports games, your choice. I'll be your player 2.

THIS COUPON ENTITLES YOU TO ONE:

A DAY OF YOUR PICKS

Pick the food, the TV, and anything else you want.

THIS COUPON ENTITLES YOU TO ONE:

UNINTERRUPTED NAP

No time limit.

THIS COUPON ENTITLES YOU TO ONE:

A DAY WITHOUT CHORES

I promise to step in.

THIS COUPON ENTITLES YOU TO ONE:

CAR WASH

Terms: To be delivered within 24 hours of receiving the request.

THIS COUPON ENTITLES YOU TO ONE:

WEEKEND GET-AWAY

You get to choose when and where.

THIS COUPON ENTITLES YOU TO ONE:

SLOW DANCE

And whatever happens after... ♡

THIS COUPON ENTITLES YOU TO ONE:

DAY TO SLEEP IN

Terms: Can be redeemed only on weekends.

THIS COUPON ENTITLES YOU TO ONE:

FOOT RUB

Just relax and enjoy!

THIS COUPON ENTITLES YOU TO ONE:

PLATE OF HOMEMADE COOKIES

Terms: Let me know 24 hours in advance if you have any special requests.

THIS COUPON ENTITLES YOU TO ONE:

STRIP
TEASE

And whatever happens after...♡

THIS COUPON ENTITLES YOU TO ONE:

CANDLE-LIT DINNER

Terms: To be delivered within 48 hours of receiving the request.

THIS COUPON ENTITLES YOU TO ONE:

CONTROL OF THE REMOTE

Beer included!

THIS COUPON ENTITLES YOU TO ONE:

"YES"

ALL DAY

Terms: Can be redeemed only
on weekends.

THIS COUPON ENTITLES YOU TO ONE:

AFTERNOON ADVENTURE

Terms: To be delivered within a week of receiving the request.

THIS COUPON ENTITLES YOU TO ONE:

BIG
CUDDLE

No time limit.

THIS COUPON ENTITLES YOU TO ONE:

A FANCY DINNER AT A FANCY RESTAURANT

You can pick the place or let it be a surprise!

THIS COUPON ENTITLES YOU TO ONE:

PIZZA AND

MOVIE NIGHT

You can pick the movie, of course! Drinks included!

THIS COUPON ENTITLES YOU TO ONE:

KNOCK-YOU-OF YOUR-FEET KISS

And whatever happens after... ♡

THIS COUPON ENTITLES YOU TO ONE:

....

....

TERMS & CONDITIONS:

CAN BE REDEEMED ONLY ONCE.

CANNOT BE EXCHANGED.

NON TRANSFERABLE.

With Love

THIS COUPON ENTITLES YOU TO ONE:

....

....

TERMS&CONDITIONS:

CAN BE REDEEMED ONLY ONCE.

CANNOT BE EXCHANGED.

NON TRANSFERABLE.

With Love

THIS COUPON ENTITLES
YOU TO ONE:

....

....

TERMS&CONDITIONS:

CAN BE REDEEMED ONLY ONCE.

CANNOT BE EXCHANGED.

NON TRANSFERABLE.

With Love

THIS COUPON ENTITLES
YOU TO ONE:

....

....

TERMS&CONDITIONS:

CAN BE REDEEMED ONLY ONCE.

CANNOT BE EXCHANGED.

NON TRANSFERABLE.

With Love

THIS COUPON ENTITLES YOU TO ONE:

....

....

TERMS&CONDITIONS:

CAN BE REDEEMED ONLY ONCE.

CANNOT BE EXCHANGED.

NON TRANSFERABLE.

With Love

THIS COUPON ENTITLES YOU TO ONE:

....

....

TERMS&CONDITIONS:

CAN BE REDEEMED ONLY ONCE.

CANNOT BE EXCHANGED.

NON TRANSFERABLE.

With Love

THIS COUPON ENTITLES YOU TO ONE:

....

....

TERMS&CONDITIONS:

CAN BE REDEEMED ONLY ONCE.

CANNOT BE EXCHANGED.

NON TRANSFERABLE.

With Love

THIS COUPON ENTITLES YOU TO ONE:

....

....

TERMS&CONDITIONS:

CAN BE REDEEMED ONLY ONCE.

CANNOT BE EXCHANGED.

NON TRANSFERABLE.

With Love

THIS COUPON ENTITLES YOU TO ONE:

....

....

TERMS & CONDITIONS:

CAN BE REDEEMED ONLY ONCE.

CANNOT BE EXCHANGED.

NON TRANSFERABLE.

With Love

THIS COUPON ENTITLES YOU TO ONE:

....

....

TERMS & CONDITIONS:

CAN BE REDEEMED ONLY ONCE.

CANNOT BE EXCHANGED.

NON TRANSFERABLE.

With Love

Made in the USA
Columbia, SC
11 December 2024

49071376R00046